P9-DGH-027

Cath Kidston® in print

Brilliant Ideas for Using
Vintage Fabrics in Your Home

Photographs by Pia Tryde

CHRONICLE BOOKS
SAN FRANCISCO

contents

introduction

Ever since I was a small child, I've had an intense fascination for print. Although my memory is terrible for many things, such as telephone numbers, I can recall every print throughout our house as I was growing up: the striped rose bedroom curtains, the magnolia print in our playroom, the lilacs in the spare bedroom, and so on. The same goes for clothing: my favorite strawberry-print sundress, the rainbow-colored stripes on my sand shoes, and, of course, my first psychedelic pantsuit.

I began buying vintage prints as a teenager, when it was popular to trawl flea markets for "granny" dresses. It was also a time when many great contemporary fashion designers were in their heyday—Laura Ashley, Celia Birtwell for Ossie Clarke, and, of course, Biba and Kenzo. Sadly, I neglected to save anything from that time, but each of these designers has proved to be hugely influential over the years.

As I became involved in interior design, I began seriously to collect vintage fabric. I have an enormous respect for all things original, so reusing an old pair of draperies, rather than buying something new, appealed to me. Alongside the interior decorating, I started a business dealing in old fabrics and found there were some great vintage prints around. In the early eighties, the taste in interiors was for ornate, overblown "country house" decoration, which has never appealed to me. I prefer a much fresher look, still using these great old floral prints but placing them in a much cleaner, more contemporary setting. The concept for my present business was born.

In my first shop, I sold colorful painted furniture and lots of secondhand fabrics. I had a vision of whitewashed walls, freshly painted furniture, and cheery cabbage rose fabrics with minimum fuss and frills. Inspired by my childhood nursery—with its gloss-painted pale pink walls, linoleum floor, and oversized chintz chair covers—I sought to reinvent this look for a modern space. I like things that have a practical, utilitarian feel to them, so the idea of a floral-print ironing board cover, a plastic-coated tablecloth, and even a shopping bag appeals much more than designing any amount of heavy swags, cascades, and Austrian shades. I began to take vintage document prints and rework them into what I saw as contemporary floral prints in new, fresh colorways and with bolder layouts.

Once I began selling ironing board covers, the business really took off, and the fun began: thinking up a range of products for the store. Now we sell more than 500 items around the world, from dog beds to bath towels, hair ties to handbags. I still collect old prints—it is a compulsion I am sure will never leave me—and the fabrics provide me with new ideas each season.

I hope this book provides inspiration for others, just as seeking out and working with wonderful old prints stimulates me. Since I am hopeless at sewing, many of the ideas included here are very simple, be it cutting up brushed cotton pajamas into dust cloths or covering a brick with funky retro florals to use as a doorstop. If you are lucky enough to be able to sew, the possibilities really are countless; if not, there are always people who can help. As far as I am concerned, my main enjoyment is in inventing endless ideas for using print—often with surprising and impressive results!

big florals

big florals, for me, are the epitome of a classic print. A huge bunch of roses or a combination of cottage garden flowers, such as hollyhocks and delphiniums, set against white or a washed-out background color, immediately springs to mind. But there is a very fine line between this kind of print looking rather sad and gloomy and its having a wonderfully cheery effect, which is nearly always down to color. It doesn't matter how old the fabrics are or what variety of flowers they depict, just as long as the palette has a freshness to it. Anything too muted and autumnal will look dull, while even the most traditional flower design in great colors can look really contemporary.

Vintage prints from the thirties and earlier are some of the best, with beautifully hand-painted flowers in vibrant colors. Because of their age, they tend to be fragile and are therefore hard to find. Many of my favorite prints are colorful designs from the fifties, such as classic roses, and if you are lucky, you can still find reasonably large pieces. There are plenty of oversized floral prints available today, often copies of archive designs. I am often disappointed by how few have that winning combination of color and print that really works, but there are some good ones to be found. When you buy new fabric, you may find it worthwhile to wash it down to give it more character, or sometimes even to run a pale-colored dye through it. Washed blues, greens, and pinks often succeed in giving a fabric a fifties feel.

Uncluttered rooms are where I prefer to use big floral prints, in quite a simple way, rather than mixing them with other patterns. I loathed the "country house" look of the eighties, when rooms were smothered in print and felt really claustrophobic. If a design is strong enough, it will stand out well in a room on its own. Draperies made in an oversized floral print can sometimes look too traditional, whereas a chair cover made in such a fabric always seems to work. A simple tablecloth looks good in a big floral, as does a single splash of print used for a headboard or bedcover. It is also fun to make something unexpected, such as a beanbag, in a really traditional floral fabric.

Remnants and small lengths of big floral prints can be used up in all sorts of ways. A pair of bold printed pillowcases look great contrasted with white bed linen. Stiff lampshades are easy to recover with fabric; straight drum shades work well, as they have a modern style to them. Even a single bunch of flowers from a flower design stretched over a frame can make a perfect picture.

beanbags

are incredibly comfortable, which is why I like them so much, but all too often they are covered in garish prints. I found this beanbag in our attic, left over from our child's playroom, and re-covered it with a piece of old-fashioned French chintz. It has replaced an armchair in our spare bedroom, where it has added an element of fun in what was quite a serious-looking room, as well as offering our guests a quiet place to relax. By choosing an existing beanbag, I kept the sewing to a minimum; this way you can slip the new cover over the old beanbag and not have to worry about making an additional lining. Some beanbags are made from a simple round top and bottom, joined by a straight panel. Others, like the cover shown on pages 10–11, are made from a single piece of fabric that is sewn into a tube and then stitched with six or so large darts at either end to form a point. Either way, the beanbag is sewn with simple seams (see page 156). When sewing the last seam, however, you must remember to leave a large opening either to slip the new cover over the existing bean bag or to fill it with beads. As beanbags often get dragged across floors, I would recommend using a reasonably hard-wearing fabric, such as linen, to withstand any wear and tear.

seat cushions

can revive tired armchairs, giving a new lease on life with a fresh splash of print. The feather cushion on this chair was worn out, but instead of re-covering the whole thing, I replaced just a single cushion and then had an extra scatter cushion covered in the leftover fabric. The same could be done to a worn-out sofa, perhaps even using different prints for each seat cushion to create a kind of patchwork effect. For more complex upholstery jobs, I use a professional seamstress, but if you are a relatively competent sewer, you might want to tackle a simple shaped seat cushion yourself (see page 159). Don't forget that if you have just enough fabric for the top and front edge of the seat cushion, you can always make the underside and back with another fabric in a solid color.

garden kneelers

are not often great looking. I bought mine, with its original basic plaid top and waterproof base, from my local garden center. To give it a facelift, I hand-sewed some floral-print cotton over the top of the plaid; it is so much easier to customize an existing kneeler than to make one from scratch. Cut your chosen fabric to the size of the top plus seam allowance, turn and press a hem to the wrong side on each side, and then neatly sew in place by hand (see page 156). I have used a bright white sewing thread to contrast with the deep reds and greens of the floral print. A bright fabric, such as a printed corduroy, would be perfect; look for old skirts in junk shops. An avid gardener would love this for a gift, wrapped with a pair of gardening gloves or a book.

pretty aprons

were almost obligatory in the fifties; something to show off over an outfit while you served dinner. There are some amazing vintage pinafores, with crazy prints, lacy trims, and all sorts of pockets, ruffles, and other details, to be found in secondhand stores. If nothing else, they look great hanging on the back of the kitchen door. To make your own apron, decide whether you prefer a retro waist-tie apron or a classic cook's pinafore, like the one shown here. I often keep it simple and use lengths of cotton tape for the waist ties, instead of making them. To finish, add one or two practical patch pockets (see page 156).

tablecloths

are the perfect way to show off those big, bold floral designs that were so popular in the fifties, especially if you lay them over long refectory tables or use them outdoors, where they can really make an impact. It's fun to accentuate any unexpected mixes of colors by teaming a tablecloth with mismatched napkins in primary colors or pastel, ice-cream shades. Just to add to the riot of color, seat your guests on a selection of vivid gloss-painted chairs. A plain tablecloth is the easiest project to sew if you're a beginner; stitch simple hems along all sides of a piece of fabric cut to size (see page 158). That's it! It doesn't even matter too much if your seams aren't perfectly straight; this just adds a little homespun charm.

24

delicate chintzes

are a little impractical, but they are irresistibly pretty and often
cheap to pick up. This small piece of floral chintz cotton
fitted perfectly into an old picture frame that I found at a tag
sale, but it would look equally good under glass as a
bedside tabletop, where it wouldn't suffer any wear and tear.
Decorative picture frames tend to come in dark wood, but they can
be transformed easily with a couple of layers of pale chalky paint
and a top coat of wax polish.

fifties florals

make delightful slipcovers for bedrooms. I inherited this very tall, shaped headboard, which I re-covered in this striking, oversized rose print. To keep everything in proportion, I raised the bed itself onto a wooden platform; not only does this create excellent storage space underneath, it also gives the bed a rather grand, stately look. Apart from a couple of printed silk scatter cushions, the covered headboard provides the only pattern in the room; I deliberately left the walls a plain pale turquoise as a counterpoint to the vibrant red and yellow rose print. Here, it was important to choose a bold floral, as a more muted print might have looked rather old-fashioned. I have corded the seams on the front of the cover shown here (see page 158), which can be a little tricky when sewing around curves. Just take your time, and carefully baste all the seams before stitching for a neat finish.

laundry bags

in basic white cotton or linen can be given added interest with appliqué flowers cut from scraps of print (see page 157). This is really easy to do. Once you have cut around the flowers, lay them on the bag and either pin or baste them in place. Alternatively, stick them down with a light squirt of photographic spray adhesive. This will hold the appliqué in place perfectly while you sew it to the bag using small, neat slipstitches. I left the edge of this appliqué raw and used a matching sewing thread, but you could also hem the patch or use a different-colored thread for contrast, provided your sewing is really neat.

29

bedrooms, such as

this studio room, can be simple spaces with little else but a mattress or futon on the floor. I love the fact that these two different prints are the only form of decoration in this otherwise all-white bedroom. The combination of dots and cabbage roses lends this room a warm, friendly feeling, despite its apparent emptiness. Teaming dots and florals in an otherwise white space gives a contemporary edge to the prints, while the fabrics help to soften an uncompromisingly modern room.

lampshades

are the perfect way to use up any small scraps of a favorite fabric, since you need only a tiny amount to wrap around a frame, and this can then be sewn in place (see page 157). With this pair of bedroom lamps, I have indulged myself by adding feather butterflies to the frilly shades, but I make sure that they are kept well away from the lightbulbs, so as not to be a fire hazard.

practical
bedcovers

are essential for any pet owner, as muddy paw prints are so often a problem. In our household, my dog, Stanley, has a habit of dashing upstairs after his nighttime walk and leaping straight onto the bed. A "blanket cover," which gets washed every week, is the answer. I have a huge selection of prints I use in our bedroom, but this large piece of unlined chintz is a favorite. There is no need to line the cover—leaving it unlined makes it easier to launder—so just finish it with simple stitched hems (see page 156). Depending on the size of your bed, join two or more widths of fabric, taking care to match the pattern, until the cover is the width required. Look for patterned flat sheets that you can also use in this way—the ultimate no-sew bedcover.

lined drawers

are rare these days, as many people can't be bothered with the fuss, but the joy I gain from using this immaculately lined chest of drawers is tremendous. I had only a couple of rolls of this hand-blocked rose-print wallpaper, so rather than paste it on a wall, I paid someone to professionally line a cherished chest of drawers. Even if you simply pin down some wallpaper or giftwrap with thumbtacks, it is well worth doing.

practical prints —oilcloth,

adhesive-backed fabric, terry cloth—are some of my favorite fabrics, despite being made for specifically utilitarian, rather than decorative, purposes. While lengths of vintage fabrics are quite hard to find, there are numerous sources of new practical fabrics, provided you know where to look. The fun is in thinking of alternative ways of using them.

Terry cloth printed in stripes or florals is always worth looking for. There is a wide selection around; large department stores are a good place to look. Striped beach towels make an ideal pair of bathroom curtains and look equally great in a kitchen or utility room. I recently made a slip cover for an armchair from some dotted terry cloth, which works particularly well in a child's room. Street markets are always my first stop when I am on vacation. I have found some great cheap towels in Italy and Spain, such as an enormous rose print, which I made into giant terry-cloth cushions. They are ideal for lounging outdoors or in a sunroom, but also make great floor cushions. Unusual washcloths are also worth collecting. I keep a pile of them, all in different prints, in a big bowl in our bathroom, and they look great all together.

Oilcloth is another of my favorite fabrics; its glossy coating gives any print a modern twist. Its traditional use is for tablecloths, but it is an ideal upholstery fabric. Prosaic kitchen chairs and stools can be transformed with shiny seat cushions, but it is also fun to use oilcloth on grander pieces of furniture. I recently covered a pair of nineteenth-century French bedroom chairs in rosy oilcloth. If you are re-covering antique furniture, I recommend getting it done professionally. My upholsterer covered our chairs immaculately, finishing the edges with traditional brass nails. I have also made an instant tabletop by covering a piece of particleboard in oilcloth, using a staple gun, and setting it on a basic trestle base painted in white gloss. This is a great way to make cheap tables for a party. It's fun to use a different print for each table.

Old-fashioned hardware stores are a good place to rummage around for adhesive-backed fabric in wonderful patterns. You may find some basic checked, plaid, and marbled prints, or even some retro kitchen-utensil designs or florals. Their traditional use is for drawer lining, but a great print stuck over a tabletop not only looks good but wears well. Leftover scraps are ideal for covering cookbooks. Most of these old-fashioned, utilitarian fabrics are really cheap to buy, but the effects can be startling when they are used well.

wipe-clean tabletops

can easily be created using self-adhesive plastic-coated fabric, which not only is excellent for lining kitchen drawers but makes a pretty work surface, too. Adhesive-backed plastic is still very popular in continental Europe, so I often pick up a few rolls from hardware stores when I am on vacation there. You can find some great old-fashioned vegetable prints and florals, as well as the ever-popular gingham checks. When sticking the fabric down, work across the table from one side to the other. Personally, I don't worry about any wrinkles, but if you want a perfectly smooth surface, ease out any air bubbles as you go, because they can form creases that are hard to remove later on. Once the adhesive-backed plastic is stuck down, trim off any surplus.

upholstered steps, painted

in white gloss and given an oilcloth top in one of my own modern floral prints, have found a home in my bathroom. This robust, hardworking fabric can be put to all sorts of uses besides tablecloths: I have used oilcloth to reupholster kitchen stools, chairs, and even worn-out car seats (see page 159). The high-gloss coating on the fabric really brings out the colors of a print, giving it a modern edge.

way-out washcloths made from pure cotton printed with unusual diagonal stripes in strong shades are irresictible. I buy them in bulk, in as many colors as possible. I love the combination of all these bright cotton washcloths, so I pile them up together in a dish in my bathroom.

45

pop-print towels

can be made from retro terry-cloth curtains, with just the minimum of sewing (see page 158), just as bathroom curtains can be made from a pair of bath sheets. As much as I love a completely plain bathroom, I cannot resist using printed terry cloth. It's fun to layer pattern upon pattern: I team this loud seventies floral with a more traditional rose-print hand towel, which I picked up in a street market, and my own dotted fabric. Seventies pop-print designs are hard to find in any great quantity, but if you are lucky enough to get hold of a reasonable length, they make the most perfect slipcovers for bathroom chairs. Nowadays, you can find some great contemporary designs that take on a new light once transformed into curtains or upholstery.

bathrooms come in all shapes and sizes;
I am lucky to have a room large enough to hold a free-standing rolltop bath
tub, which sits underneath a large window. I prefer to keep bathroom

fixtures white, and to introduce color and pattern with the odd hint of printed fabric. Terry cloth is the natural choice for a bathroom, because of its high absorbency, and comes in a huge range of colors and patterns. Another trick is to trim white towels with a favorite ribbon.

tea towels

are ideal projects for beginner sewers to use for practicing their sewing-machine skills. Any old cotton or linen fabric will do, cut to size and stitched with a basic straight hem. Add a hanging loop made from ribbon, or sew a tie from any leftover fabric (see page 158). Homemade tea towels, tied with raffia or ribbon, make an ideal "granny gift."

dust cloths

are my latest obsession! I prefer to recycle fabrics, whenever possible; so any suitable scraps of printed brushed cotton—even old pajamas—I cut into squares and reuse in a flash. This pink pictoral print is far too garish to be made into children's clothing, but it is absolutely ideal for the cleaning bucket. Dust cloths are a fabulous no-sew project, as you don't even have to stitch any hems; simply cut the fabric with pinking shears to create a zigzag edge, or leave them frayed, as I have done here.

gift boxes

are a great way of utilizing otherwise strange prints. This dogtooth check with roses was really rather ugly as a large piece, but cut down into small scraps and glued in place to cover matchboxes, it comes into its own. A bundle of covered matchboxes tied up in an acetate bag make an excellent inexpensive gift. Or use the box as packaging for tiny, precious presents, such as a pair of earrings or a brooch. If you are covering a matchbox, remember to leave the strike strip uncovered.

drum lampshades

, for some reason, are excellent when covered with an unusual print. I had this material in a drawer for years and was never quite sure what to do with it. But when I needed a shade for this bright yellow lampbase, it really came into its own. It is easy to cover a basic drum shade using nonflammable spray glue, so long as you cut the fabric to the exact size (see page 157). Add only the smallest amount of fabric for a hem, because if you fold over too deep a hem, it will show through when the light is switched on.

57

abstract prints

abstract prints are still easy to pick up and well worth looking for, despite the fact that they are becoming increasingly fashionable. There are famous designs by artists such as Lucienne Day, which are expensive and collectible. They tend to appear at better auction houses and are a serious investment, not to be chopped into cushion covers. Because I know little about this era, I am always cautious about cutting fabric up for cushions without looking at the seams. Fabrics are normally named along the edge if they are by a famous studio or artist, so it really is worth checking before you get out the scissors. Then there are the more everyday graphic designs from the fifties and sixties, which have been made into curtains or draperies and chair covers and which I come across in thrift shops and tag sales. These are worth snapping up.

Framed fabrics can look terrific. A large piece of print in the right colors, stretched over a canvas frame, makes a wonderful picture. Likewise, some of these vintage designs in unusual color combinations would look hideous furnishing today's homes, but they can work really well for fashion. Recently, I bought a piece that was black with khaki and lime green squares and made this into a really chic tote bag. The same goes for satin upholstery prints from the fifties in geometric designs, which make great evening bags. If you see an interesting print but are not sure what to do with it, snap it up; an idea will always come along later.

Graphic florals, particularly those from the seventies, are coming back in, yet they are still cheap to pick up. Look for swirly flowers in psychedelic colors at thrift shops and garage sales. Internet auction sites are a good hunting ground for this kind of thing, but check what kind of fabric you are buying. Polyester-cotton is best avoided, but it was quite common in this era, particularly for duvet covers and curtains.

Used sparingly, a little print goes a long way. One of my favorite projects in this book is the doorstop on page 67, covered in a funky floral linen. I recently looked through some old seventies decorating books; the prints were hideously overpowering as curtains, draperies, and wallpapers. That said, I recently took a pop print from my own collection and had the design painted onto my trailer. It caused quite a stir on its way to the Glastonbury (pop music) Festival. I guess there is something about these big, bold prints out in the open air that simply brings a smile to the face!

wall hangings

made from framed abstract textile designs make wonderful pictures. Although this style of print has become very sought after, the occasional retro print can turn up in thrift shops. This yellow "atomic" print was originally made into a pair of typical fifties short curtains. Since these designs are becoming very collectible, it is best not to chop them up too much but to hang one entire drapery panel as a painting, stretching the fabric like a canvas over a wooden frame (see page 159). You can buy ready-made stretchers from art-supply stores, but these come only in standard sizes. Otherwise, you can go to a picture framer who will make a stretcher to order, tailor-made to fit the piece of fabric. It is best to attach the material to the frame with a staple gun, rather than nails or tacks, as this minimizes the amount of damage to the fabric.

outdoor living,

whether it is in a trailer, tent, or garden shed, needs to be a perfect hideaway. I use my trailer as a home office: it was useless setting up my laptop on the kitchen table at home to work, as within minutes I was distracted. This old trailer provides the perfect solution. Redecorated inside and out and now parked out of the way in the garden, it is my sanctuary. Inside, the desk has a picture-window view over the fields, and I have plenty of space for filing and shelves. What's more, it can be used as a spare bedroom, or better still, taken on vacation! I love the flowers painted on such a huge scale and long to decorate an old car in the same way.

doorstops

can be cheaply made by covering a standard builders' brick in a striking pop print. The brick needs to have some padding, such as table felt, wrapped around it first to prevent it from chipping, but the fabric just needs to be sewn simply by hand (see page 157). I chose this seventies fabric because it has a rather cheeky, cartoonlike quality, but almost any print will work, so long as it has a darkish ground, since the doorstep cannot be cleaned. They make great inexpensive presents; the weight only adds to the surprise, once the doorstop is gift wrapped.

workboxes

and other fabric-covered boxes often turn up at antique markets. They are worth snapping up, as they make excellent storage, particularly the ones with drawers and compartments. I now have a collection for my sewing kit, ribbons, and buttons. All the clashing prints look great together on a shelf. If you can't find vintage boxes or want to use a particular print, you can easily cover a simple shape, such as a shoe box, yourself.

69

tote bags work

well made from graphic seventies prints (see page 158). The antique metallic ribbon used for the handles contrasts with the abstracted florals. There are all sorts of ribbons around, from natural burlap to colorful stripes, that would work well as handles. They just need to be heavy enough so the handles don't curl.

mini florals

are some of the prettiest fabric prints. Although they are usually designed for clothing, they can easily be adapted for home furnishings. It is still possible to buy fabulous vintage designs—rolls of old shirting and lingerie prints sometimes turn up at antique fairs—but there are also some great new designs on the market. The London department store Liberty's is famed for its floral prints, but many dress-fabric stores have a good selection of old-fashioned floral prints.

Delicate, tiny florals are ideal for either making or trimming bed linens. These small-scale prints are often found on very fine cotton, which is perfect for bedding. When trimming pillowcases, I tend to make two mismatching pairs. I put four pillows on a bed, with each pair trimmed in a slightly different way.

Combine these small florals with other prints, such as classic gingham. I have made cushions from tiny floral prints that I have teamed with a gingham check backing. Likewise, I have teamed a pair of gingham check curtains with a floral fabric valance. Other prints on a similar small scale, such as baby polka dots and classic shirt stripes, are also good foils for mini florals.

Strips of mini florals, cut on the bias for bias binding, make a great trim or piping, which can be applied to cushions or wool blankets. The strip also looks great around the hem of a skirt. Leave the edges of the piping frayed and stitch it to the right side for a really vintage look, or even layer one print on top of another.

Secondhand stores often yield some of the best prints, in the form of old shirts, aprons, and housecoats. Since these garments are often dreadful shapes, you don't need to feel guilty about chopping them up. The beaded necklace shown in this chapter was made from an old housecoat. The small scale of these designs makes them ideal for tiny items such as little coin purses, coat hangers, and lavender bags. I had fun covering an old pair of shoe trees, but pretty much anything works in this kind of print.

Basic projects are all I can manage in the sewing line, but I have advertised in a local store for a dressmaker. I am hopeless at following a pattern or copying other garments, but when I have known exactly want I wanted and given clear instructions, the results have been great. There are some exquisite printed silks around, which are ideal for clothing, so it may be worth trying to make some simple garments or accessories.

old bed linens are ideal

for customizing with floral-print patches. Vintage pillowcases are cheaper when bought as singles, as everyone is after pairs, but there is no unwritten rule that all bed linens have to match. Patching pillowcases in different ways but using the same fabric helps to tie together mismatching linen (see page 156). Here, I have added one thin strip of print to the cuff of one pillowcase and a central panel to the other. Even a small square of print in one corner looks good.

ruffled curtains

are the perfect partner for a short fabric valance. This style of window treatment has been out of fashion for a while. However, I love the look of them, so when I found this old-fashioned chintz valance minus its draperies, I made a pair of simple curtains in a basic red gingham (see page 158) to go with it. I love the way the light shines through the fabric, although I have also hung a plain white roller shade with blackout lining fabric at the window to block out the light in the morning. The simple gathered ruffles that edge the curtains echo the gentle gathers of the valance, which unifies the look, despite the different prints.

zip-up purses

, when made with an extra waterproof lining, make excellent cosmetic bags. These Eastern European prints are traditionally red and white or blue and white toile, but any scraps of faded florals will look great together. You could even mix two different mini-floral prints within one purse (see page 159).

handmade
gifts
have a special quality. There are endless simple products to make from scraps of old fabric. Traditional items, like lavender bags, are always popular, but it is fun to think up something unusual. It can be easier to customize an existing product than to start from scratch. Here, I have covered some old shoe trees to give as a gift along with a pair of my own-design slippers (see page 158). The challenge is to always come up with something new!

ironing

on a table is a luxury, provided you have the space. My grandmother had a big old washroom and always had an ironing table out instead of a board. The secret is to heavily pad the tabletop with interlining or an old blanket and then cover it with cotton using a staple gun (see page 157). It is best to use a heavyweight cotton, as any fine fabric will wear out quite quickly. The prettier the print, the better—anything to cheer up such a dreary job!

silky camisoles,

like the one shown here, can be made from lengths of old printed silk, which are quite easy to find. Silk is perfect for making into clothing, but since I can't follow a dressmaking pattern, I have to pay someone to sew things for me! Local newspapers are the ideal place to look for a dressmaker; or you could put an ad in the window of a local store that allows this form of advertising. The easiest method of making an original garment is to trace the shape of the pieces from a favorite garment; keep it as simple as possible (see page 156).

simple bags

, such as this envelope shape, are just right for holding jewelry. It is relatively easy to make, as it doesn't require a fastener; it just needs to be deep enough so you can fold over the top flap. Children's dress cottons are usually an ideal scale of print for this kind of small bag. The same shape will also work as an evening clutch bag, but you will need to use a stiff brocade or cotton so it is firm enough to hold its shape.

88

beads

covered with tiny scraps of fabric can create some fantastically bold jewelry. I found this mini-floral print on an old cleaning smock and knew it was the perfect allover design to cover some wooden beads (see page 156). I love the eccentric mix of the floral print, plastic, and metal beads threaded together to make this necklace. This fabric would also have made a great corsage or hair tie.

rubber gloves

are synonymous with the most boring household chores, yet they are an essential item. I like to customize this type of basic utility product (see page 158). Decorated with a brilliant yellow floral, these gloves bring a smile to my face whenever I see them dangling over the faucets in our utility room!

pictorial prints are always

included in my collection of vintage fabrics. I so admire the skill of the designers; their draftsmanship is often incredible. But it is the eccentricity of some of these retro designs that appeals to me. It is something that you rarely see in fabric prints today.

American prints are some of the best I have come across. Apart from classic cowboy designs, which inspired me when I first began to make my own designs, I have found fabrics with subject matter ranging from spacemen to beauty parlors. I have also found some great designs in Britain; these tend to appear at car boot (garage) sales and on Internet auction sites. Very occasionally old rolls of pictorial wallpaper turn up, too; these are worth snapping up as they are increasingly hard to find. Even a single panel on a wall can look good.

These prints often work best in children's rooms. A pictorial print fabric laid under a glass tabletop is ideal for a bedside table. Some prints can frame up well into pictures. A lot of these designs are scenic, and you can cut a number of different images from one print to make a great set of pictures. You can even do this by cutting up cheap polyester-cotton bed linen sets emblazoned with cartoon characters, which are for sale all over the place.

Cushions are similarly an ideal use for this kind of print. With old fabrics there is usually not much to go around, so I use a plain backing, which also helps to set off the print. Children's fabrics are good for beanbags or floor cushions, and corduroy makes a practical choice to go with them. If you don't have much material, you can just put a square of the design as a centerpiece on a larger cushion.

Obvious uses for specific prints often present themselves: a great dog print simply had to be made into a pet bed for my terrier, Stanley. Other prints can be harder to place, but are worth buying and holding on to if they are a great design. A few years ago, I bought some spaceman fabric that I absolutely love, but I just couldn't make up my mind how to use it. It was only when I was redecorating my husband's office that I found its perfect home: as the upholstery on his desk chair.

cushions

for kids' rooms are the perfect place to have a little fun. There are some superb pictorial fabrics around that are just right for basic cushions (see page 156). I love this French farmyard scene, particularly the cute sheep in the corner, but I had only a small piece. Taking one of my favorite sections, I hemmed the print into a square and applied the fabric panel to a polka-dot cushion. Dot prints are an ideal fabric for children's rooms as they have an enduring, uplifting quality.

97

tabletops

of plain glass placed over prints frame and protect the fabric. This cowboy print is preserved under glass as the top of a homework table. It is the perfect place to tuck in favorite photographs, which we add to over time. Bamboo bedside tables and bathroom storage often paint up well and are ideal for taking a glass top; check that they are not too wobbly before buying.

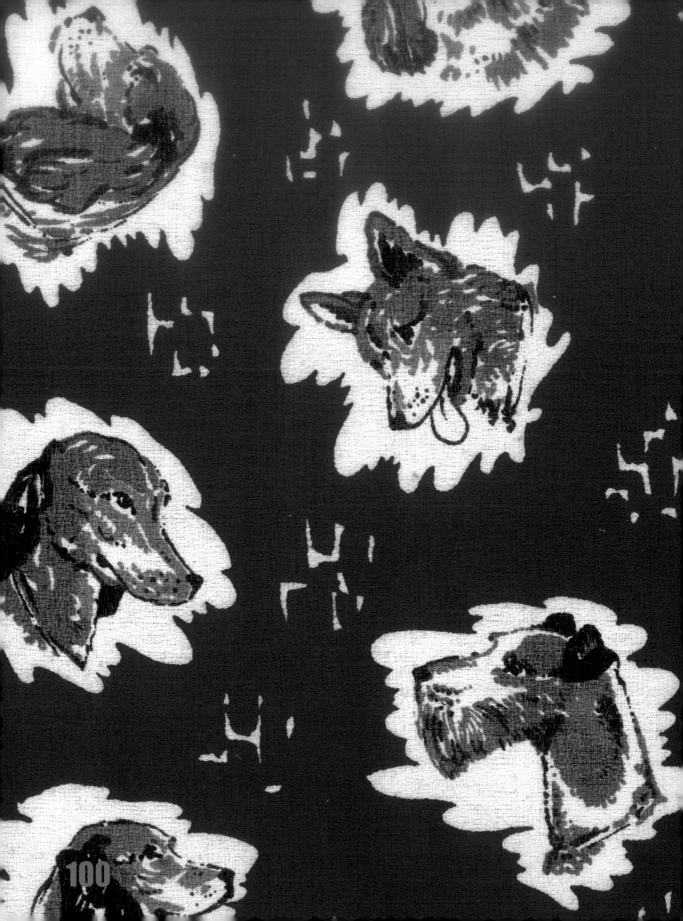

pet beds

take a lot of wear and tear, so they need frequent laundering. The bed on which my terrier, Stanley, sleeps is a large square cushion, so it is really simple to make a slipcover to fit—so simple, in fact, that Stanley has a choice of covers in prints ranging from old roses to polka dots (see page 156). I couldn't resist making an extra cover from this dog print fabric. He seems to like it, too.

office chairs and children's pictorial
prints may seem an unlikely pairing, but, for me, this fabulous spaceman

print is the perfect upholstery fabric for an otherwise serious room.
I was lucky enough to find a whole drapery panel, so there was sufficient
fabric to have this chair professionally re-covered for a look that is out of
this world!

cushion covers
are quick to make and can be easily changed to give a room a different look—this is particularly useful in a child's room, as you can change their bedroom subtly as their tastes mature. All too often, kids want something new, which is why I reckon it is best to keep more expensive items, like curtains, plain. This boat print seemed to me ideal for a child's room, so I made it into basic cushions (see page 156). I have kept the style simple, without any fancy piping or trims, so that the nautical print, complemented by the polka dot backing fabric, can take center stage.

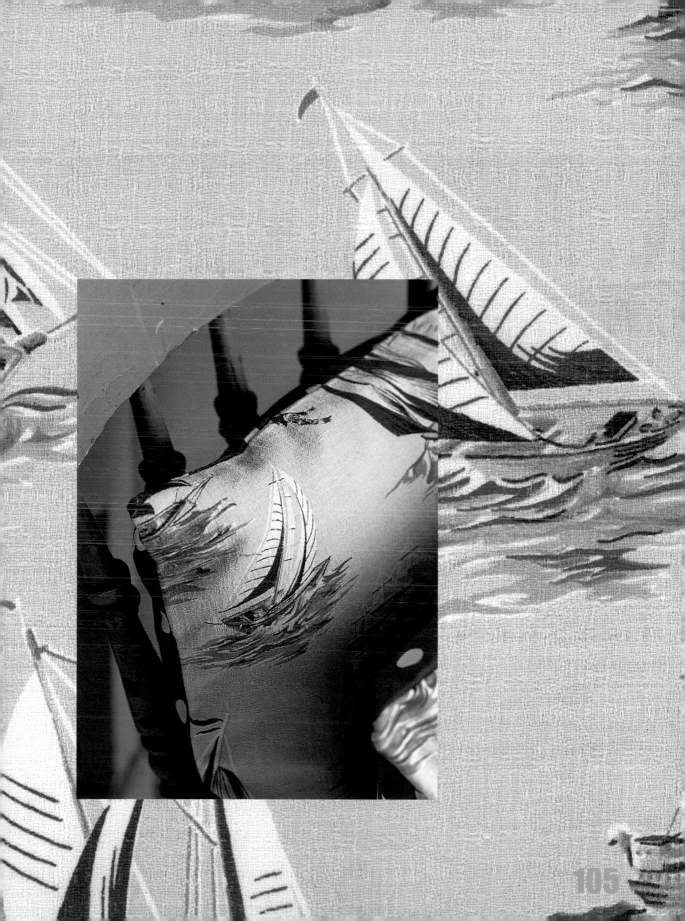

framed fabrics

can be a good way of showing off either small scraps of a favorite print or a precious vintage piece that you don't want to cut up. This sweet toile was ideal for cutting up into pictures, as each scene could be framed separately. The same can be done with cartoon-character fabrics, which are easy to buy as duvet covers. Even cheap modern ones work well when they are put into the right frames.

LONDON BRIDGE
OCTOBER
Until 30 October add 1 hour for BST

High and Low Water

	Time	m		Time	m		Time	m		Time	m
1 F	0322 0951 1529 2214	7.27 0.62 7.23 0.63	**9** Su	0255 0936 1610 2236	2.12 5.23 1.81 5.54	**17** Su	0327 1004 1539 2228	7.29 0.77 7.40 0.63	**25** M	0531 1138 1829	1.11 6.62 0.35
2 Sa	0354 1017 1601 2232	7.06 0.79 7.08 0.86	**10** Su	0442 1103 1723 2337	1.86 5.58 1.64 5.98	**18** M	0405 1032 1621 2255	7.03 0.88 7.15 0.89	**26** Tu	0015 0640 1232 1922	7.14 0.74 6.11 0.99
3	0424 1039 1632 2252	6.80 0.92 6.86 	**11** Tu	0541 1155 1819	1.47 6.07 1.02	**19** Tu	0446 1104 1707 2327	6.64 1.03 6.74 1.20	**27** W	0104 0731 1317 2005	7.36 0.54 7.17 0.14
	0453 1103 1707 2319	6.54 0.97 6.59 1.02	**12** Tu	0022 0634 1145 1911	6.45 1.14 6.5 0.71	**20** W)	0533 1145 1805	6.20 1.22 6.29	**28** Th ○	0145 0813 1356 2042	7.37 0.50 7.02 0.34
	0524 1748 2354	6.28 1.02 6.25 1.17	**13** W	0100 0725 1314 1957	6.86 0.90 6.93 0.48	**21** Th	0011 0630 1237 1915	1.52 5.82 1.43 5.99	**29** F	0221 0849 1430 2112	7.28 0.55 6.72 0.57
	0504 2312 2337	5.97 1.19 5.85	**14** Th ●	0138 0810 1350 2041	7.16 0.75 7.21 0.49	**22** F	0112 0743 1355 2035	1.80 5.66 1.56 5.97	**30** Sa	0254 0918 1502 2134	7.14 0.63 7.13 0.76
		1.48 5.60 1.50 5.47	**15** F	0214 0853 1426 2120	7.34 0.69 7.39 0.33	**23** Sa	0242 0904 1543 2158	1.87 5.78 1.32 6.23	**31** Su	0323 0944 1533 2156	6.97 0.73 7.00 0.88
		1.88 5.27 1.82 5.32	**16** Sa	0251 0930 1501 2157	7.38 0.70 7.47 0.43	**24** Su	0412 1026 1715 2314	1.54 6.13 0.83 6.70			

key rings

are an easy project for children to make, particularly if you cover over an existing fob. If an adult cuts the material to size, then all the child has to do is place it over the fob and sew around the edges with simple running stitches (see page 157). This tiny scrap of horse fabric seemed ideal for my pony-obsessed goddaughter to use.

patchwork

patchwork originated as the application of patches to conceal worn areas of old clothing and furnishings. From there it progressed to joining patches of old but still good fabric to form a new fabric and, finally, to the complex quilt designs we know—an art form in its own right. But even old-style "patchwork" has its charms. A textile dealer friend who sold highly fragile antique fabrics rhapsodized over the patches used to repair the materials she sold.

Worn-out chair seats and arms can be successfully repaired using patches. Recently, I needed to rescue an old armchair that was threadbare in places, but the original cover was really quite special. Rather than re-covering the entire chair or trying to match the original print, I patched it with another contrasting floral fabric. I then made an extra scatter cushion in the new print to complete the patchwork effect—with delightful results. I have since repaired an eiderdown and cushions in the same way, using a contrasting printed fabric.

Patchwork quilts I find irresistible. For years they have been a minimalist's nightmare, being evocative of cute country cottages. But it depends on how they are used: they look best in fairly plain rooms. They are ideal for throwing over the backs of chairs or sofas to brighten up a bland room. While I like the classic faded sprigged prints characteristic of most old patchwork, there are some terrific bright-colored ones available. I have vintage patchworks from India in clashing hot pinks and oranges that have totally transformed my living room.

Layering prints, much like combining them in patchwork, runs the risk of looking too cluttered, if lots of busy prints are put together. Again, it helps when the room itself is quite plain. I have successfully combined two printed tablecloths on a big kitchen table. I also love the piles of clashing printed notebooks on my desk, where there are no other patterns around.

Combining lots of different prints to make your own patchwork projects is easy. I recently bought some great girls' dresses made from bordered tablecloths, which had been sewn together with the borders forming stripes. This idea would work equally well for cushion covers. Strips of print can be added to ready-made solid-colored items, from skirts to pillows. Often they look good when the colors clash. The fun is to take random colors and patterns and throw them all together as if by accident!

living rooms

my favorite vintage patchwork throws from India provided
the color scheme for my living room—a clashing combination
of hot pink, orange, and yellow. I've deliberately kept the walls
a calm cream and free from pattern to provide some contrast.

gift wrap

can easily be made from your favorite fabric prints with just a basic scanner and printer attached to your computer. Simply scan a piece of fabric in and print it out on paper! If you have a basic knowledge of computers, it is relatively straightforward to change the colors or alter the scale of the design. I often print out large sheets of print on my industrial printer at work, but even regular letter-size sheets are useful in an emergency.

patches

add character, especially when sewn on by hand (see page 156). I just love the delphinium print upholstery on this chair, so I rescued it by covering the threadbare arms and seat with patches of another bold print. Hand-sew the patch in place as carefully or as roughly as you like. Here, adding a cushion covered in the same fabric as the patches brought it all together, making a feature of the two striking prints.

patchwork quilts

are really coming back into fashion and make perfect throws for armchairs and sofas. Damaged ones are cheap to pick up, and they are ideal for cutting up and making into cushion covers (see page 156). Or you can throw one over a sofa, where any blemishes will not be noticed. Traditional gingham and shirting stripes are usually a good choice for mixing with floral patchwork or can be used as backing fabrics for cushions where extra is needed.

dining rooms

layering these two tablecloths was really a happy accident—
a single cloth on its own wasn't long enough to cover my
dining table, so I used two. I was delighted with the effect.
You could add to the mix-and-match vibes by using napkins
in the same fabric as the underneath cloth.

kids' clothing

made from recycled tablecloths are such a neat idea.
I found this selection at a stall on Portobello Road,
a regular street market in West London. The print and
the colors are so much better than any new fabrics
available. There are some good basic patterns for
children's clothing: something like a simple A-line skirt
(see page 157) is easy to make, even if you have never
attempted any dressmaking before.

123

notebooks

covered in patterned papers are a passion of mine, picked up at school, which I can't shake off. One of the highlights of my school vacation, before the new term started, was visiting the local stationers to stock up on books and papers. All these patterned papers were bought in a small village in Italy, where the shop owner still kept stock from thirty years ago. I particularly like the Rasta-colored paper juxtaposed with the garden roses.

books, books, books

faded florals

faded florals gain in character as they age. Even the most worn-out print can have a use. I recently bought a huge piece of fabric—even though it was disintegrating—simply for the inspiration I gleaned from its muted color palette. It was very fragile and full of holes, but a friend suggested using it to line a linen closet. It suited that use perfectly, and once it was glued on with a fine layer of photographic spray adhesive, the holes only added to its crumbling character. I have also made lengths of delicate fabrics into panels and screens, which are ideal uses for fragile pieces. And if something is really damaged, it can always be patched with another, similar fabric, which can add to its character.

Washed-out, pale colors are restful in a bedroom. There is nothing quite like a faded floral chair cover or eiderdown cover, but it is hard to find new fabrics that have the same appeal. It is best to avoid those fabrics with a fake vintage effect. You can, however, achieve this look with modern fabrics. If you have the patience, leave your fabric out on the clothesline over summer. After a period of time—depending on how strong the sun is—it will fade naturally. Although there is nothing like natural sunlight to do the trick, you can gradually bleach fabrics on a hot wash with some biological detergent. However, it does take quite a few tries to achieve a proper washed-out look.

Staining fabrics with tea is another useful trick; natural fabrics, such as cottons, linens, and wool blends, work best for tea dying. Fill a dishwashing bowl with hot brewed tea, removing the tea bags, and submerge the fabric. Stir the contents of the bowl continuously with a wooden spoon, or the fabric will stain unevenly and look blotchy. Once the fabric has soaked and is the color you want, remove it from the bowl, and rinse it through with plenty of warm water and a little mild dishwashing detergent. Alternatively, you can run a pale fabric dye through larger lengths of material in the washing machine. It is best to start with a very weak solution and build up the color with a second wash, if necessary.

Pastel shades are pretty, too, and can be cleaner than some faded florals. To freshen up a bathroom, try combining pale turquoise with pink or washed lime with canary yellow in funky floral prints—great for a young girl's bedroom.

antique lace

in silver silk added to both ends of a length of
floral muslin made a perfectly pretty shawl to wear
to a party. The minimum sewing was needed, but
the effect makes quite a statement. Muslin is an
excellent handkerchief or scarf fabric, and very
easy to sew by hand. Long, thin scarves are useful,
as they double up as a belts to wear with jeans.

lined closets

are exactly the sort of "hidden extras" that I'm all in favor of. For me, it turns an otherwise mundane domestic chore, like putting away the laundry, into a secret pleasure. The material I used to line this linen closet was terribly old and frail, but it doesn't matter; the holes and fading add to its character. I used photographer's spray adhesive to cover the closet interior and pasted up the fabric, working quickly before the spray glue dried. The original uninspiring basic pine interior was transformed by the fabric lining.

customized clothing has a unique

appeal, being completely original. The patches added to this cardigan, on the elbows and front, give decorative interest to an otherwise plain garment and save darning any worn elbows. I find it easier to sew on patches than darn to wool, so I add them to woolens and T-shirts (see page 156).

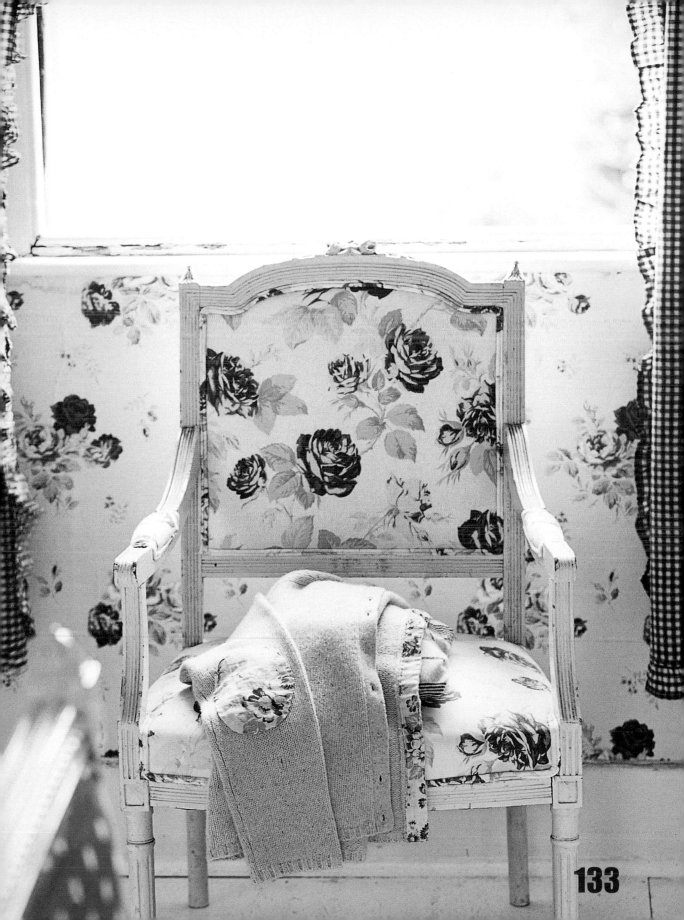

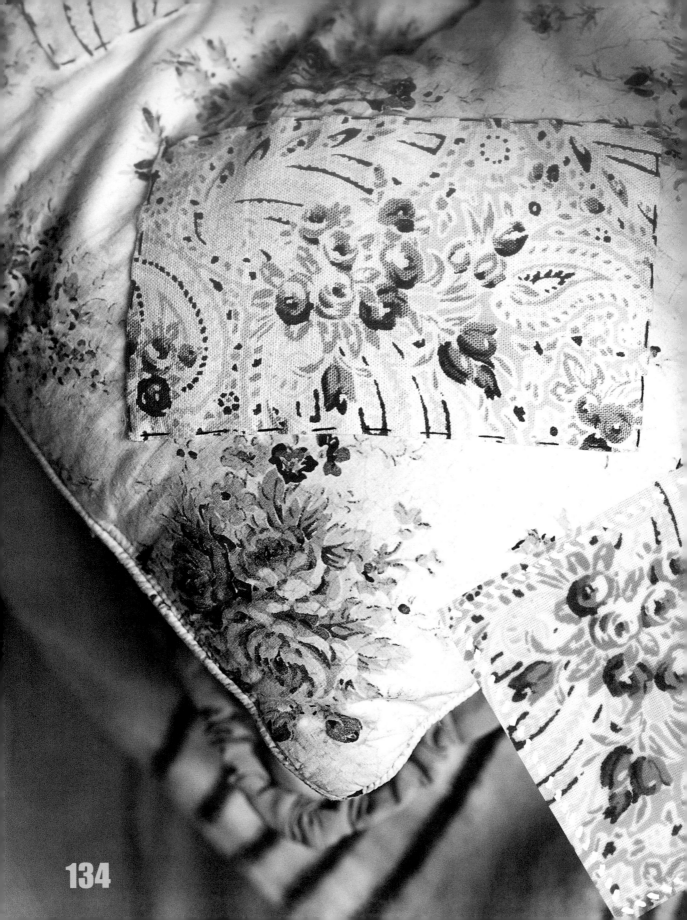

feather eiderdowns

are the coziest thing, but they are becoming increasingly hard to find and often need repairing. This one was leaking feathers, but rather than try to disguise the holes, I patched it up in a really obvious way. Each patch was sewn on using a contrasting colored thread, so the fabric squares form a pattern of their own (see page 156). I chose this fabric, as it wasn't too dominant when layered on top of the original eiderdown, but you could go for a clashing contrast.

placemats

and napkins couldn't be simpler to make (see page 158). I prefer to hand-sew them, as the uneven stitching has more character. They can be made from odd scraps of material. You don't have to make a matching set; you just need to choose prints of a similar character. Don't forget to put some cork, wicker, or a heatproof mat underneath, if you need to protect your tabletop.

wall hangings

are a great way to display fabrics, particularly large-scale prints, which often take on a completely different character once framed (see page 159). There are some wonderful "Tree of Life" designs around. These tend to look rather old-fashioned as upholstery but look much better when used flat, either within a shade or as a decorative panel. It is worth looking for old Indian cotton bedspreads with this sort of print, as they make perfect panels to hang above a bed in place of a headboard.

painterly florals

with a true hand-drawn quality are just magical, so it is worth considering how to use them to their best advantage. Some of my favorite painterly prints are surface printed and hand-blocked wallpapers, to which the color is applied by hand. There are companies that still use these methods to print wallpapers; although they are expensive, they are real works of art. If you are commissioning a short run of wallpaper, you can choose your own colors. I am about to decorate my bathroom using a hand-printed paper. It is a large, airy room with plain white cabinets and bathroom fixtures, and a shiny white linoleum floor, so the only decoration will be a bright rose-covered paper.

Examples of vintage wallpapers sometimes crop up. Snap them up to use as wonderful drawer linings or even as a single panel on a wall. If it is a big print, it can really dominate a room.

Treasured lengths of material are best suited to making into cushions, as you tend to take a pattern in at a relatively close distance. Make them up simply, with, at most, a simple braid or bobble fringe, and set them against a plain chair or sofa cover. Very bright, colorful prints of this kind are great outdoors and excellent for garden furniture. If you are lucky, you can sometimes come across old parasols with this sort of design.

Show off a particular favorite print by making it into a tote bag; I guarantee it will get a lot of use and be much admired. I have a couple of bags made from classic rose prints, and they are the one thing people always stop and ask me about. Some of the best painterly prints can be found on old fifties sundresses and summer skirts. For me, the problem is that they never fit because they all have such tiny waists, so chop them up. However, a really pretty party dress will look great left out on display, just hanging on the back of a door.

The bright color combinations used in many vintage prints often surprise me. Some of the classic fifties florals are in outrageous colorways: clashing oranges and pinks with accents of black. When used sparingly, they can add that special element of surprise to a room.

shopping bags are classic, especially

when made up in an irresistible vintage print. Tote bags are very simple to sew, but are best made of a sturdy fabric (see page 158). The more they are washed, the better they become, as they seem to mellow with age. Old furnishing prints that would look gloomy on a sofa work really well when converted into a bag.

colorful cottons

combined with inexpensive wool fringe gives a cushion a lovely summery feel (see page 156). I use this cushion, made from an old sundress, outdoors on a painted cane chair. As is often the case, this kind of fringe looks better once it has been washed.

144

pretty
boxes

and old cake tins are always worth collecting. I use them to package gifts, such as homemade cakes. I lined this beautiful cardboard box with crisp pink tissue paper and filled it with chocolates, but an old-fashioned tin with an iced sponge cake inside always goes down well. I cheat by buying cakes at my local farmers' market, but I have given up pretending I make them myself, since I usually get caught!

flower prints make the most fabulous

cushions and often need just the plainest of backings. This exquisite dahlia print looks better with a solid color on the back, so I have used a basic white linen to make up these cushions. I have added a white bobble fringe for a bit more character (see page 156). You can still buy crocheted cotton lace in some dress-fabric stores, which is a good alternative trim.

useful information

where to shop

antique fairs and markets
Search for the details of local antique fairs, markets, and auctions in magazines; or search the Web for fairs in your state. Vintage clothing fairs are good places to hunt for fabrics, as they are often attended by textile dealers. Look for well-known markets, such as the Scott Antique Market, held once a month in Atlanta and also (November through April) in Columbus, Ohio. Some of the best fairs are held outdoors, usually early in the morning at venues such as racecourses, agricultural show grounds, and old airfields.

estate sales and thrift shops
This is where you can find real bargains. They usually have an area dedicated to textiles, so it is easy to dash in and out during your lunch hour. If you find nothing at first, don't be put off. Stock changes pretty quickly in thrift shops and is unpredictable, so when you do come across something good, it is all the more satisfying. I appreciate the recycling aspect of shopping for secondhand fabrics, and if the money is going to charity, that is an added bonus.

151

garage sales
In England, where I live, the equivalent of the American garage sale is the car boot (trunk) sale, a regular communal event with many sellers and buyers. Finding a garage sale takes a little more planning, but can be well worth the effort. You may have to riffle through piles of old clothes, but these may yield amazing fabrics that simply don't come up at antique markets at great prices. To keep track of garage sales in your area, visit www.garagesalehunter.com.

street markets
Whenever I am abroad, I always check out the local street market. The stalls to look for are those selling bed linens and terry cloth, dressmaking fabrics and kitchen wares. I have bought pillowcases, tablecloths, yards of great printed fabrics, and drawer lining papers, for example. It is also worth visiting local markets at home. They can be an excellent source for basic fabrics such as gingham.

old-fashioned hardware and fabric stores
These kinds of stores are becoming increasingly scarce—pushed out by huge centers and department stores—but they can offer some real finds. Hardware stores are good for adhesive-backed plastic and oilcloth, but look for old-fashioned tea towels, placemats, and napkins, too. Fabric stores may have bolts of vintage materials, so it is worth asking whether they have old stock tucked away. There are many more of these types of stores in Europe and farther afield. I have just been in Morocco, and the sewing shops there had an amazing range of fabrics. It is best to find the areas where the locals shop, rather than visiting the tourist markets.

local newspapers
Check out your local newspaper for charity sales and fairs. There are nearly always great bric-a-brac stalls at these events. I have bought good ready-made items, such as covered coat hangers, homemade jam with fabric lids, and fragrant lavender bags. There are always great homemade pies and cakes, if nothing else! Local newspapers are also a good place to find the details of dressmakers and upholsterers. In the past, I have placed advertisements in a local shop window and found excellent sewing help this way.

internet auction sites The Internet really has changed the way we shop. Browsing an Internet auction site, such as www.ebay.com, is now one of the easiest ways to track down vintage fabrics. I have discovered if I tap my own name into an eBay search, a mass of floral prints comes up with the description "very Cath Kidston." It has been quite a challenge to buy items under a pseudonym. You have to be really careful when buying fabrics sight unseen. So much stuff looks good online, but quite a lot of it isn't original—simply "vintage stye"—and actually quite expensive for what it is. It is always worth asking the fabric content and checking the condition things are in before placing a bid.

online shopping Like many retailers, I offer a mail-order service through my website. My own design fabrics and products are available to buy online, just click on www.cathkidston.co.uk.

tips for successful shopping

- Always go on the first day of a two-day fair. Not only do most of the best things go first, but a lot of dealers leave before the second day. The "Trade" entrance fee will cost more, but it is worth it.
- Ask for a trade discount. Most dealers will automatically offer about 10% off; you just have to ask!
- If you go to an early morning fair, take a flashlight! It can be absolutely pitch dark when they open, especially in winter, and the best bargains are to be had when people are unpacking.
- Take lots of small change and dollar bills. People are always short and often accept a deal if you proffer the exact amount.
- It can often be cold—especially, of course, in winter. Fingerless gloves are a must in the winter so you can pick things up without taking your gloves off!
- Always unfold and examine textiles. Dealers can be ruthless in hiding holes and stains.

sewing tips

making your own pattern Whether you are sewing a slipcover for a chair or copying a favorite camisole top, create the pattern by pinning each section of the item to a sheet of newspaper and drawing around the shape to be cut out. Remember to add a seam allowance all the way around each piece.

preparing your fabric Before cutting, wash your fabric at the correct temperature for its fiber content; then run an iron over it. This makes cutting easier and more accurate.

pinning out pieces When laying out all the pattern pieces on your fabric, follow the straight grain, unless they are to be cut on the bias. If your fabric has a bold print, such as a plaid or stripe, line up the pieces so patterns will match up.

cutting out pieces When cutting out your fabric, cut carefully around each paper pattern piece.

joining pieces Pin and baste the pieces of fabric together before stitching the seams. Remove all the pins before stitching.

pressing pieces Before continuing your sewing, press each seam, hem, and dart. Place your iron and ironing board or table nearby when you are ready to begin stitching. Test a scrap of your fabric for pressing before you begin to sew. Each seam, no matter how short, should be pressed as soon as it is stitched. Then the piece that will be joined to it will lie flat.

neatening threads Neaten your sewing by cutting off all stray threads.

sewing techniques

running/basting stitch Tiny running stitches can be used for seams that receive little strain. Fasten thread with a knot or couple of backstitches, then take the needle in and out of the fabric, making stitches as small and even as possible. Fasten with backstitches. For basting—holding fabrics together temporarily before stitching—use large running stitches. Fasten thread lightly at the end. To remove, cut thread at short intervals, then gently pull it out. When basting delicate fabrics like silk, use a fine thread, to avoid marking the fabric.

backstitch Fasten the thread and make a running stitch. Now take a stitch back, placing the needle in the work at the beginning of the first stitch and bring it out one stitch length ahead. Continue in this way.

slipstitch This is used to join two folded edges or to hem a folded edge. When joining folded edges, take small stitches in each edge alternately, keeping the thread within the folds. When hemming, pick up only one or two fabric threads of the single layer, then take the needle a short distance through the folded edge. Take another tiny stitch in the single layer, opposite the point where the needle emerged.

plain seam Zigzag-stitch along any raw edges to finish, either before or after joining the seams. Pin and then baste the fabrics with right sides facing. Remove the pins and machine-stitch. Remove the basting and press open.

plain hem Turn the hem to the wrong side to the required depth, press, and stitch. Alternatively, turn $1/2$in to the wrong side and press. Then turn the hem over again to the required depth and pin or baste. Press. Stitch hem close to the first fold.

hand-stitched hem Fasten the thread under the fold of the hem; take a tiny stitch, catching a thread or two of the fabric under the fold; and bring the needle through the edge of the fold. The stitches should be small and even and slightly slanted.

overcast stitch Hold the edges to be sewn together. Take the stitches over the edges diagonally.

gathers Leaving a long loose thread end at the beginning, work running stitches along the length of the fabric; secure the end with backstitches. Then slide the fabric along the thread until the gathered edge is the desired length. Secure the loose thread end by winding it in a figure eight around a pin. Adjust the gathering as required. If attaching a ruffle, pin or baste the ruffle to the fabric with right sides facing (ruffle upside down), and stitch. Turn the ruffle over, and topstitch close to the seam.

ties Fold the fabric in half lengthwise, with right sides together, and pin or baste. Stitch along two sides, leaving one end open for turning. Trim the corner. Turn right side out. The blunt end of a pencil can be used for pushing the ends through. Fold in the raw edges of the open end of the ties for neatness before attaching. For pointed ends, stitch and cut at an angle of 45 degrees.

darts To shape an item, such as the beanbag on page 10, stitch a dart. With right sides of the fabric together, mark a v-shaped dart with a ruler and chalk. Fold the fabric between the marking in a straight line to form a point. Pin. Baste the dart from the point to the widest part. Stitch the dart from the widest part to the point. If the dart is more than 5/8 in wide, slash and press open. Otherwise press darts downward.

bias binding Cut strips of fabric across the bias (on a diagonal fold). Lap the strips so the fabric threads are aligned, and seam where the edges cross. Stitch the strips together to form long lengths. Fold and press the edges to the center of the strip. Trim any extending corners. Stitch the binding strip and fabric along hem edge with right sides together. Turn the binding over the hem edge; turn under the raw edge of the binding strip and hem to the machine stitching on the inside.

reinforced stitching Attach a tie, loop, or handle by stitching the ends in a square pattern. Then stitch across the square on both diagonals. Repeat for an extra-secure finish.

corded seams Cover a length of filler cord with a strip of bias binding, and stitch close to the cord, using a zipper foot on the machine. Place the covered cord between the seam edges with corded edge inside the seamline and all the raw edges together. Pin, then baste in place. Stitch on the seamline, again using the zipper foot, close to the cording.

mitered corners To make a neat point at a corner, first turn the seam allowance to the wrong side, and crease. Fold the point in, diagonally across the corner where the creases meet. In bulky, heavy fabrics, most of the corner should be trimmed away. Turn on creased lines, and baste folded edges. Press.

overlapping corners Turn up a double hem on two opposite sides of the fabric; pin, baste, and stitch in place by hand or machine. Repeat on the two adjacent sides. Where the second hems overlap the first, slipstitch (see page 154) the edges together.

patch pockets Turn in the seam allowance at the top of the pocket. Turn a hem at the top to the outside and stitch ends. Turn and press side seam allowances in. Turn hem to inside enclosing seams. Slipstitch (see page 154) hem in place. Turn under point at bottom of pocket. Turn and press remainder of the seam allowances along the pointed bottom edge. Baste pocket to garment, and topstitch close to edge, pivoting needle at corners. For curved pockets, clip at the curves so the pocket will lie flat.

project instructions

appliqué patches (see pages 16, 75, 117, 132, and 135) Cut a piece of fabric to the size of patch required, adding a ³/₈ in hem allowance to each edge. Turn a ³/₈ in plain hem (see page 154) to the wrong side of each edge, taking care at each corner, either mitering them or overlapping them (see page 155). Handsew the fabric patch to the item using small, neat running stitches (see page 154).

beaded necklace (see page 89) Cut small rectangles of fabric the size of each bead plus a little extra. Apply fabric glue to each bead, and stick on fabric patch. Fold any excess fabric in at top and bottom of each bead; alternatively cut small v-shapes out of edges to minimize excess. Once glue is dry, string beads onto a length of cord or a thin fabric tie (see page 155) to make into a necklace or bracelet.

beanbag (see page 12) When using an existing beanbag as a template, trace the pieces onto your fabric, adding ⁵/₈ in seam allowance. When starting from scratch, cut two circles of fabric to desired size, adding ⁵/₈ in seam allowance. Measure the circumference of one circle, and cut a side panel to this measurement by the height required, again adding ⁵/₈ in seam allowance. Join the ends of the side panel by sewing a plain seam (see page 154). Lay one circle of fabric right side up, and place the side panel over the top, right side down, aligning the raw edges. Pin and baste. Join with a ⁵/₈ in simple seam. To attach the bottom circle, lay it right side up and align the remaining raw edges of the side panel, right sides down, around the perimeter. Pin, baste, and then stitch together, leaving a gap to insert the filling. Turn right side out. Fill with polystyrene beads, and close the opening using small, neat overcasting stitches (see page 155).

bedcover (see page 35) Cut your fabric to the desired size, adding 2in hem allowance. If necessary, join two or more widths of fabric with 2in plain seams (see page 154) to achieve the size of bedcover required. Turn under 1in on both ends twice, press, and baste. Turn in both sides in the same way, mitering the corners (see page 155). Stitch close to the edge of the folds.

camisole (see page 84) Using an existing camisole as a template, trace all the pieces onto your fabric, adding ³/₈ in seam allowance. Cut out pieces and zigzag-stitch all raw edges. If necessary, sew a dart (see page 155) in each side of front to shape. With right sides together, pin and baste front to back along side edges. Stitch with ³/₈ in simple seams (see page 154). Make thin shoulder straps, using method given to make ties (see page 155). Stitch each strap in place, on corresponding points of front and back. Turn right side out. With right sides together, pin and baste a lace trim around the top and bottom edges, as shown on page 84. Stitch with ³/₈ in seams. Open out the seams, and topstitch on the right side of silk, close to the seam edge.

cook's apron (see page 18) Trace the pieces onto your fabric, making the bib (top) approximately two-thirds the width of the skirt (bottom) and gently curving the sides of the bib out to meet the outside edges of the skirt and adding ³/₈ in hem allowance. Cut out. Sew a ³/₈ in plain hem (see page 154) along each edge, taking care when sewing around any curves. Make two ties (see page 155) for the waist and one tie for the neck strap. Add one tie to each edge of the apron at the waist, using reinforced stitching (see page 155). Stitch each end of the neck strap to the top edge of the bib, making sure that the strap is not twisted. If you like, finish by adding patch pockets (see page 155) just below waist level, matching up the prints.

cushion cover (see pages 96, 101, 104, 118, 144, and 149) For the front panel, cut a piece of fabric the size of the pillow form, adding ³/₄ in seam allowance. For the back panels, cut two pieces. Cut the first the same height as the pillow form and half its width, adding $3/4$ in seam allowance to the top, bottom, and outer side edge and $1^1/4$ in to the inner edge. Lay each back panel right side down, and turn under a double $3/8$ in hem on each inner edge; pin, baste, and stitch. To add a trim, place the front panel right side up, and pin and baste the trim around the edges the desired distance in from the seamline, folding the trim 90 degrees at the corners; stitch in place. For cording, follow instructions for 'Upholstered chair cushion' (page 156). To complete cover, place the two back panel pieces on top of the front panel with right sides facing and raw edges matching, so that the hemmed edge of the wider back piece overlaps that of the narrower one by $3^1/2$ in. Pin and baste, then stitch around the outer edges. Turn cover right side out, and insert pillow form.

doorstop (see page 67)

Wrap a standard builder's brick in some protective padding, such as table felt. Glue in place. Cut a piece of fabric large enough to wrap all the way around the padded brick, with enough on either edge to cover the sides, adding $5/8$ in seam allowance. With the wrong side out, wrap the fabric around the brick, pinning it in place, tailoring the cover to fit snugly down all four corners but leaving an open flap on the bottom. Remove the cover from the brick and baste the pinned side seams. Stitch (see page 154). Trim excess seam allowance. Turn cover right side out, and place it over the brick. Turn under hems on all three sides of open flap, and slipstitch to the sides all the way around to close (see page 154).

ironing table (see page 82)

Cut a piece of table felt or a blanket the size of your tabletop, adding enough to fold over the sides and turn to the underside of the tabletop. Cut a piece of heavyweight cotton slightly larger than the size of the padding. For securing the material to the table, follow the method given for stretching fabric over a frame to create a wall hanging, using either tacks and a hammer or a staple gun.

key ring (see page 109)

Cut piece of fabric to size required to cover store-bought key fob, adding $3/8$ in seam allowance. With right sides out, glue the fabric to the key fob using fabric glue. Using running stitches (see page 154), hand-sew around each edge. Trim any excess fabric to finish.

kids' clothing (see page 122)

To make a simple A-line skirt, cut two pieces of fabric for front and back, making top edge at least 5in larger than waist and bottom edge approximately one-third wider than top edge. With right sides together, pin and baste pieces along sides. Stitch with $3/8$ in plain seams (see page 154). Turn and press $3/4$ in to wrong side twice around top edge. Pin and baste. Stitch, leaving a small opening at center front for threading elastic through. Attach end of length of $3/8$ in-wide elastic to a safety pin, and thread through waistband. Knot elastic together at when waist is required size. Stitch across opening. Try on skirt and pin hem at required length. Turn, press, and stitch plain hem (see page 154) at bottom edge of skirt.

lampshade (see pages 32 and 56)

Cut a length of fabric the dimensions of the shade, adding $3/8$ in hem allowance. Using non-flammable spray glue, stick the fabric to the shade, overlapping the ends and turning $3/8$ in hems to the inside at top and bottom edges. Make sure the hems are not too deep, as they will be visible when the lamp is on. For the ruffled shade shown on page 32, make a gathered ruffle (see page 155) to fit the circumference of the shade, and stitch around the bottom edge. Feather butterflies, bought from notions departments can be held in place, away from the lightbulb, with glue or a couple of small hand stitches.

laundry bag (see page 29)

Cut a piece of fabric twice the desired width of the bag by the height, adding $5/8$ in seam allowance. With right sides together, fold the piece in half widthwise. Pin and baste seams along bottom and side edges. Stitch a plain seam (see page 154) along the bottom edge taking $5/8$ in seam allowance. Stitch the side seam, stopping $1^1/2$ in short of the top edge. At the top edge, turn $1/2$ in to the wrong side and press. Turn another 1in hem and press. Pin and baste close to the edge of the folds along the hem to make the channel for the drawstring. Stitch. Thread a length of cord through this channel, or make a long tie (see page 155) to use instead of cord. To add an appliqué, cut out your preferred print, then pin and baste in place on the bag. Attach to the bag with topstitching.

rubber gloves (see page 91) With pinking shears, cut a strip of fabric three times the circumference of the glove cuff. Fold and press in pleats all along the length of the fabric strip. Trim the cuffs of the gloves with pinking shears. Turn the gloves wrong side out. Pin a pleated strip around each cuff. Stitch. Pin together the ends of the pleated strip where they meet, and stitch. Turn gloves right side out.

ruffled curtains (see page 76) For each curtain, cut a piece of fabric one and a half times the desired finished width and the finished length plus the following allowances: the diameter of the curtain rod, 4in (ease around rod plus hem and heading), and 6in (lower hem). For the ruffles, cut two strips of fabric 4in wide and one and a half times the finished length. On the leading (inside) edge of each curtain, turn under $3/8$in; pin and stitch. On the outside edge, turn under $1/4$in; press. Then turn under another $3/8$in; pin and stitch. On the top edge, turn under and press $1/2$in. Then turn this edge under to a depth of 2in plus half the diameter of the rod. Pin, baste, and topstitch close to raw edge; press. Mark another stitching line, with pins or tailor's chalk, $1^{1}/4$in from folded top edge; pin, baste, and topstitch or hand-hem in place. Stitch around all edges of ruffles with zigzag stitch. Turn under $3/8$in on short ends and one long edge. Pull up gathers to fit finished length of curtain, and adjust fullness evenly. Pin and baste just under hemmed inner edge of curtain. Topstitch in place.

shoe trees (see page 80) Cut two circles of fabric to wrap around the toes, adding $5/8$in hem allowance. Turn and press a $5/8$in hem around each circle. Hand-sew running stitches around edges of each circle. Place fabric circles over shoes trees, and draw threads of running stitches to gather fabric around toes. When fabric is gathered tight, fasten off. Tie a length of ribbon into a bow around each shoe tree to conceal the gathering stitches.

slipcover for headboard (see page 26) Trace the contours of the headboard to make the pattern pieces, and transfer to your fabric, adding $5/8$in seam allowance. Cut out. Using a solid-colored fabric for the back, trace and cut out another piece the same size. Measure the perimeter of the front panel, minus the bottom edge, and cut a side panel to this measurement by the depth required, adding $5/8$in seam allowance. If you have enough fabric, cut out and join strips of bias binding to make cording (see page 155). Lay the front panel right side up, and cut a piece of cording to the perimeter of the panel, minus the bottom edge. With raw edges aligned, pin and baste the cording to the outside edge. With right sides facing, pin the side panel to the front, taking care to pin it right into the corners. Stitch with $5/8$in seams. Clip the seam allowance around the corners to ease the seams. Attach the back to the side panel in the same way, leaving the bottom edge open. Turn right side out. Sew a plain hem (see page 154) all the way around the bottom edge of the cover to finish.

tablecloth, towel, tea towel, and placemat (see pages 21, 46, 50, and 137) Use the same method for each. Cut the fabric to the size required, adding 2in hem allowance all the way around. Turn under both ends by 1in twice; press and baste. Turn in both sides in the same way, mitering the corners (see page 155). Stitch close to the edge of the folds. To make a hanging loop for a towel, make a thin tie (see page 155), or use a length of ribbon. Fold in half and stitch ends together. Sew the loop to one corner.

tote bag (see pages 71 and 142) Cut two pieces of fabric to the desired size of bag, adding $5/8$in seam allowance. With right sides together, stitch plain seams (see page 154) along three sides, leaving the top edge open. Turn right side out. To make a lining, cut two pieces of lining fabric to the same size as the bag, adding $^3/_8$ in seam allowance. With right sides together, stitch seams along three sides, leaving the top edge open. Turn $^3/_8$ in hem to wrong side of open edge of lining. Press. Turn $^5/_8$ in hem to wrong side of open edge of bag. Pin and baste. For the handles, make two wide ties (see page 155) of the length required, or cut two lengths of ribbon. Pin in position, one on each side of the bag, making sure they do not twist. Stitch down each edge of the handles, using reinforced stitching at the ends where necessary (see page 155). With wrong sides together, pin and baste the open edge of the lining to the inside top edge of the bag. Slipstitch the lining in place, sewing as close to the top edge of the bag as possible.

upholstered chair cushion (see page 14) Trace the contours of the cushion top to make the
pattern pieces, and transfer onto your fabric, adding $^5/_8$ in seam allowance. Cut out. Using a solid-colored fabric for the underside, cut out another piece the same size. Measure the perimeter of one panel, and cut a side panel to this measurement by the depth required, adding $^5/_8$ in seam allowance. Join this strip into a band with a plain seam (see page 154). If you have enough fabric, make strips of bias binding to cover a length of filler cord (see page 155). Lay the top panel right side up, and cut a piece of covered cord the perimeter of the panel, plus a few inches. Pin, baste, and stitch the cording to the top panel (see page 155), beginning and ending at the center back and leaving about 2in where the cording ends overlap. Clip the cording seam allowances at the corners. Trim free cording end to overlap by 1in, and undo stitching on overlap. Trim cord ends to meet. Fold under $^1/_2$ in of bias strip, and wrap strip around other end; complete stitching. Join side panel to top panel, placing seam at center back, then attach bottom panel to side panel, leaving a gap for cushion. Turn cover right side out, insert cushion, and close gap with slipstitching.

upholstered steps or stool (see page 42) Cut a piece of oilcloth the size of the top of the step
or stool seat, adding enough extra on each edge to cover the sides of the step or seat and to turn to the underside. With the oilcloth in position, attach the fabric to the underside, using a staple gun or upholstery nails and a hammer. Pay particular attention to the corners; fold them in neatly, as you would when wrapping a parcel, trimming any excess where necessary.

wall hanging (see pages 61 and 138) To avoid cutting your fabric, buy a set of artists' stretcher strips
that make a frame at least 4in smaller than the material. Make the frame by fitting together the mitered ends of each strip. Check the squareness of the frame by measuring across the corners, ensuring that both measurements are equal. With the fabric right side down, center the frame on top. Fold one edge of the fabric over the frame and tack in the center using a staple gun, allowing 2in excess. Move to the opposite side of the frame, pull the fabric firmly, and tack with a staple in the center. Move to an adjacent side and do the same, pulling firmly and tacking the fabric to the frame at the center. Add a fourth tack on the opposite side. Moving out from the center of each long side, pull the fabric taut and tack to the frame every 2in, leaving about 2in untacked at each corner. Repeat for the short sides. Pay attention to the corners; fold them in neatly as though wrapping a parcel. Tack the corners through the folded fabric while keeping it taut.

zip-up purse (see page 79) Cut two pieces of fabric the desired size of purse, adding 1in seam
allowance (so that total width is 2in longer than zipper). Turn in 1in along one long edge of each piece. Press. With zipper facing up, place folded edges of each piece along the teeth of the closed zipper so that they almost meet in the middle. Pin and baste. Stitch along entire length. Open zipper. Fold the joined fabric pieces along zipper edge so the right sides are together. Stitch along other three edges with 1in seams. Turn right side out.

acknowledgments

All my thanks to Pia Tryde and Marco Sandemann; Andy Luckett and Kane Dowell; Jo-Ann Sanders; Karina Mamrowicz; Jennie and John Morgan; Elaine Ashton; Anne, Helen, Lisa, and Claire at Quadrille; Hugh and Jess; and the entire team at "Cath Kidston" who have all helped so much on this project.

Project Editor Anne Furniss
Creative Director Helen Lewis
Editor Lisa Pendreigh
Designer Claire Peters
Photographer Pia Tryde
Production Director Vincent Smith
Production Controller Ruth Deary

First published in the United States in 2006 by Chronicle Books LLC.

Text and project designs copyright © 2005 by Cath Kidston
Photographs copyright © 2005 by Pia Tryde
Design and layout copyright © 2005 by Quadrille Publishing Ltd

All rights reserved. No part of this part may be reproduced in any form without written permission from the publishers.

Library of Congress Cataloging-in-Publication Data available.

ISBN-10: 0-8118-5358-6
ISBN-13: 978-0-8118-5358-3

Manufactured in China

Distributed in Canada by Raincoast Books, 9050 Shaughnessy Street, Vancouver, BC V6P 6E5

10 9 8 7 6 5 4 3 2 1

Chronicle Book LLC, 85 Second Street, San Francisco, CA 94105

www.chroniclebooks.com

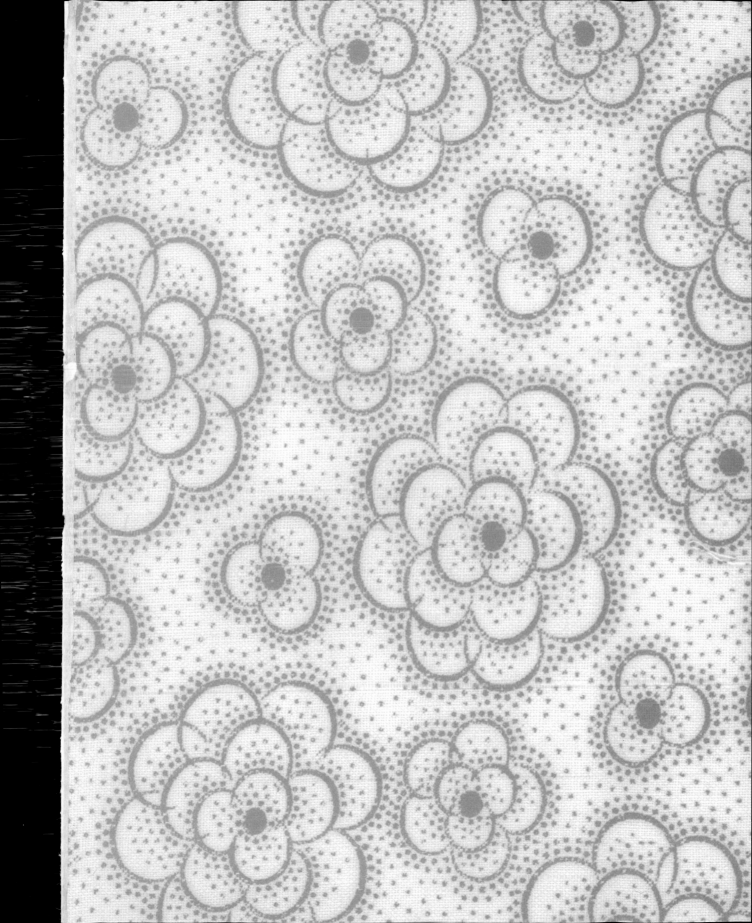